WOMEN AND
SEXUALITY

LISA SOWLE CAHILL

1992 Madeleva Lecture
in Spirituality

PAULIST PRESS
New York/Mahwah

Library of Congress Cataloging-in-Publication Data

Cahill, Lisa Sowle.
    Women and sexuality/Lisa Sowle Cahill.
      p.   cm.—(Madeleva lecture in spirituality; 1992)
    ISBN 0-8091-3329-6 (pbk.)
    1. Sex—Religious aspects—Catholic Church.   2. Women in
the Catholic Church.   3. Catholic Church—Doctrines.   I. Title.
II. Series.
BX1795.S48C34   1992
241'.66—dc20   92-914
                                                                 CIP

Published by Paulist Press
997 Macarthur Blvd.
Mahwah, N.J. 07430

Printed and bound in the United States of America

TABLE OF CONTENTS

Lisa Sowle Cahill holds a doctorate from the University of Chicago Divinity School, and is Professor of Theology at Boston College and President-Elect of the Catholic Theological Society of America. She is author of *Between the Sexes: Toward a Christian Ethics of Sexuality* (Fortress and Paulist, 1985); of *Religion and Artificial Reproduction: An Inquiry into the Vatican Instruction on Human Life* (Crossroad, 1988), with Thomas A. Shannon; and *'Love Your Enemies': Pacifism, Just War, and the Kingdom in Christian Ethics* (forthcoming, Fortress), as well as over fifty scholarly articles and chapters. She is an editor and a member of the board of directors of *Concilium,* an international Catholic theological journal. In 1984 she became the first non-Jesuit to serve as a contributor to the "Moral Notes," *Theological Studies* annual bibliographical essay on moral theology.

PREFACE

Roman Catholic tradition on women and sexuality is a
history of both oppressions and opportunities. On the
negative side, the tradition has not only been suspicious
of sex in general, but, in justifying sex primarily in terms
of procreation within the patriarchal family, it has identified women above all else by their sexuality defined as
capacity for motherhood and domesticity. Nonetheless,
I believe that Catholicism can communicate a positive
message on sexuality, including women's sexuality, by
highlighting the sociality of sex and the intrinsic con-
nections among sex, commitment and parenthood.
Much recent feminist theology rightly protests against
the Augustinian and even the Thomistic legacies, often
returning to the liberating elements in the scriptures as
a source of renewal. But it is possible as well to mine the
theological tradition for a wisdom about sex and gender
which can speak to our contemporary culture.

In the present reflections, I will first outline the
cultural context that gives a special urgency to the question of whether the Catholic perspective on sexuality
can be constructively reinterpreted today; then I will
briefly indicate both the values yielded by Catholic tradition, and the necessity of joining them with a feminist
critique (Part 1). After this introduction to the parame-

ters of the present discussion, I will develop the significance of the Catholic natural law tradition for a moral theology of sex, giving special attention to the thought of Aquinas and its positive insights into sexuality (Part 2). Then I will return to the biblical literature which has often been interpreted in a patriarchal framework, but which also offers valuable resources for a more egalitarian view of sex, and one which emphasizes its potential for intimacy as well as procreation (Part 3). Developing the contemporary problematic of an ethics of sexuality in the Roman Catholic tradition (in Part 4), I will look at ways in which the recent emphasis on "experience" in both feminist thought and official papal teaching has resulted in a much heavier stress on love or intimacy as the meaning of sex (displacing the old procreative focus). However, we shall also consider some tensions in the Catholic position, the consequences of combining an incompletely realized recognition of the equality of women and of genuine mutuality in sexual relationships, with the traditional conception of women as mothers. In the final part of this study (Part 5), I will reformulate the message of Catholicism for today in terms of an intrinsic connection among sexual expression, commitment, and parenthood, now understood in terms of relationships rather than sexual acts. I will conclude by using some of the new reproductive technologies to illustrate the significance of these united relationships for a normative understanding of sexuality.

1.
INTRODUCTION

A New Dualism?

In our culture, we are facing a new dualism about sex. The dualism of modern Western culture consists in separating the sexual body from morality, making our sexual lives not really "count" in defining whether we are good persons. Of course, following the still functioning double standard, it is much more true for men than for women that constraints on sexual behavior, except that it be contained within nonviolent heterosexual limits, are not required by our minimal expectations of moral decency.

A recent event in popular culture can illustrate my point. Witness the tragic but emblematic case of the L.A. Lakers' basketball star (Earvin) "Magic" Johnson. When the news that he had contracted AIDS hit the public consciousness with a shock last fall, there was heard widespread lament, not only because of the loss of his athletic prowess to the sport he loved and in which he excelled. Equally prominent in the media and public reaction was the fact that Johnson had been a sort of basketball ambassador by virtue of his personality, camaraderie, and generosity to fellow players, fans, and young people. His disease was perceived as especially deplorable and undeserved because he had not contracted it through drugs or gay sex, but by so-called "normal" means. "So it could happen to anyone" was the prevailing theme, giving rise to Magic's new role as an AIDS educator.

The message is that AIDS can strike anywhere, that it afflicts the unwary and even the innocent heterosexual. However, at least according to the news commentators, Magic's channel to AIDS was not through a girlfriend, or even two or three, much less a fiancée or spouse. The reports mentioned one to two hundred contacts. If a popular *female* tennis player, marathon champion, or olympic figure skater were AIDS-infected via hundreds of sexual liaisons, would she be lamented as a heroine or denounced as a "slut"? Even leaving aside the question of the double standard, it is clear that the empathetic reaction to Johnson's situation is made possible in part by a widespread willingness to say that sex doesn't really "count" (except possibly for women) in constituting one's identity as a virtuous person or a vicious one. Few would want to return to the Catholic past in which "a moral person" meant only *one* thing: sexual chastity (again, especially for women). But my central point is that if, and only if, the Roman Catholic tradition on morality can overcome the narrowness of its old focus on forbidden sexual acts, can it say something of value to a culture in which sexual acts are brought within few moral constraints whatsoever.

When Augustine, as a theologian of the church, battled his old Manicheean companions on behalf of the goodness of marriage, he repudiated their view that body and soul do not exist on the same moral plane, and that only the soul is the avenue of the good and virtuous life. According to this ancient religion, an aberration of Christianity, the soul and body are created, respectively, by good and evil divine principles. For these ancient adversaries of the Christian standpoint, body and soul existed in a state of continual warfare, optimally to be overcome by the total suppression of all sexual desire and activity. The new dualism rampant in our culture certainly does not repress the body in favor of higher spiritual aims; but just as surely as the Manicheean dualists, it views the body as not really an integral part of one's moral identity. One can be recognized as a person with a high sense of integrity in all other respects, even if one applies in the sexual realm only the norms that both partners give free consent, and that steps be taken to avoid disease. The moral significance of the body as the locus of our full personal existence is minimized in our current cultural message about sex just as surely as it was in the ancient dualist one, even though sexual activity is today glorified rather than forbidden. Part of the popular code is that one derives one's moral identity only from one's inner feelings, intentions, and consents.

VALUES OF THE CATHOLIC TRADITION

What are the basic values that Catholic ethics yields for sexuality? Most fundamentally, it validates reflection on human experience as a source of knowledge about what human sexuality means, and what its appropriate uses are. In the first place it stresses that sexuality is an *embodied* experience, not just volitional, and that embodiment means physical need and pleasure; an opportunity for the ultimate physical union of persons which can enhance affective relationship; and, last but not least, procreation or parenthood. Catholic tradition also sees sex as social, not just a matter of individual drives and pleasures, or even of the fulfillment of the couple or their immediate offspring. It is precisely in the socialization of sex that patriarchal assumptions have been immensely influential. Yet this does not eradicate the fact that sociality is an aspect of sexuality which should be recognized—and can be recognized and institutionalized in ways beneficial rather than harmful to women. Finally, the recent tradition has placed an increasingly high premium on the love of the couple. Earlier authors always recognized that sex leads to social and domestic partnership, but it has only been since the middle of the twentieth century that the intimate psychological and emotional commitment of the partners has been lifted up as the ideal rather than an occasional serendipitous benefit of what was essentially an economic relationship.

To summarize these values more concisely, we may say that the Catholic tradition holds up the value of the physical, embodied *sex* union itself; *procreation;* and *love,* all within a social as well as interpersonal context. The basic shape of Catholic ethics is established by natural law, biblical sources, and a long tradition of interpretation in the church, including not only theologians, but also official church teaching and pastoral practice.

THE FEMINIST CRITIQUE

Having previewed briefly what the Catholic Christian tradition might offer to what I view as an inadequate cultural appreciation of sex's meaning, let me also note vehemently that the Christian tradition on sexuality requires today a thorough feminist revision. The theologian perhaps most influential in setting the tone of subsequent thought on sexuality was Augustine. Although in his historical context, he perceived himself to be defending the goodness of sex and marriage against dualist heresies, he was deeply suspicious of sexual passion, was incapable of seeing men and women as equals in sexuality or anything else, and found the only sure justification of sex in procreation. Aquinas relied heavily on Augustine in interpreting both sex and women, and both theologians have been indispensable to the constitution of the Catholic tradition on women, gender, and sexuality.

2.
THE DEVELOPMENT OF THE NATURAL LAW APPROACH

Now for a more focused exploration of the basic ethical perspective which has been the background of the central contributions of the Catholic tradition on sexuality. Probably most distinctive of the specifically "Catholic" approach to ethics is the reliance on the morality of human "nature" or "natural law," the paradigm for which was provided in the thirteenth century by Thomas Aquinas. Put in simple terms, Aquinas borrowed from the philosopher Aristotle to offer a Christian version of the idea that all human beings share certain intrinsic purposes and values, and that these can be discovered by reasonable reflection on human experience itself. The meaning of sexuality derives from its procreative design, for instance, and moral norms to guide sexuality can be known by reason and are not dependent on any specifically religious revelation. In contrast to the manner in which it was later to be presented in the neo-scholastic manuals of moral theology, widely used as seminary texts in the early years of this century, Aquinas' natural law method was not rigid, deductive, or legalistic. Generalizing, rather, from behavior that he sees around him, and which he assumes characterizes the species, Aquinas states:

> Wherefore according to the order of natural inclinations, is the order of the precepts of the natural law . . . [T]here is in man an inclination to things that pertain to him more specially, according to that nature which he has in common with other animals: and in virtue of this inclination, those things are said to belong to the natural law, which nature has taught to all animals, such as sexual intercourse, education of offspring and so forth.[1]

In other passages of the *Summa,* Aquinas goes on to develop specific conclusions from general principles such as this. As he himself admits, the closer one gets to the specifics of human actions, the more likely it is that contingency and error will interfere with the universality of judgment.[2] We certainly see evidence of this in his own writings, not only in his view that women are less rational and of secondary status, but also in his view of specifically sexual matters. For instance, working from the supposition that the primary determinant of sexual morality is the physical structure of sex acts, as requiring male-female intercourse and resulting optimally in conception, Aquinas makes a distinction between those sinful sexual acts which are "against nature" and those which are "according to nature."[3] On this scale, sins which respect the procreative structure of the act are deemed less grievous than those which violate or preclude it, so that contraception, masturbation, homosexuality and bestiality would all be worse than adultery, fornication, incest and rape. Aquinas here neglects his own principle that the human faculties of reason and freedom are higher and more distinctive than physical characteristics and processes, for if the distinctively personal aspects of sex were recognized (over and above what humans have in common with animals), then certainly rape and incest would be recognized as greater sins against human dignity than contraception, masturbation, and consensual homosexuality. Moreover, this narrow adherence to a physicalist norm of "the natural" in sexual matters would hardly have been possible in a culture which respected the dignity of women as well as men, and which recognized that incest and rape are usually crimes perpetrated against females by males.

In these conclusions of Aquinas about sexual morality and gender, we see the inherent limitations of the natural law method. If its strength is its ability to make an appeal to common human values known experientially, its weakness lies in the fact that experiences will always be interpreted and values generalized from particular historical and cultural standpoints.

As far as the question of *women's* sexuality is concerned, the Catholic vision has been undeniably oppressive. This is not only or primarily because persistent notes of negativity about the value and legitimacy of sex in general have sounded throughout the writings of traditional authors. Celibacy has always been counseled as a higher choice for both men and women, and both have been instructed to confine their sexual acts within the limits of procreative intent.[4] But, to go further, the message of Catholicism (and most of Christianity in gen-

10

eral) has been of dubious value for women because sex has been intertwined at every point with issues of gender, and the gender perspective of Catholicism has been thoroughly patriarchal. As Aquinas unfortunately but not atypically put it:

> It was necessary for woman to be made, as the Scripture says, as a helper to man; not, indeed, as a helpmate in other works, as some say since man can be more efficiently helped by another man in other works; but as a helper in the work of generation.[5]

The positive values of sex have been submerged within a narrow view of women's identity as sexual beings, a view which traditionally has structured our sexuality around childbearing and domesticity. Let there be no doubt that parental and domestic roles are valuable in themselves—that is not the question here. The question is whether the importance they have for women is or should be asymmetrical to that they have for men. The definition of femininity in terms of such roles creeps into the later New Testament literature itself, an extreme example of which is 1 Timothy, probably written in the early years of the second century, when the young churches were increasingly concerned to fit into the larger social patterns of acceptability. This aim could be furthered by adopting familiar and respectable social expectations of men and women as norms for the Christian community also. The author of 1 Timothy is obviously conscious of the disruptive effects which Christian egalitarianism (Gal 3:28) might appear to have

11

on the prevailing social order, and wants to counsel church members not to pose a threat to social custom.

> Let a woman learn in silence with all submissiveness. I permit no woman to teach or to have authority over men; she is to keep silent. For Adam was formed first, then Eve; and Adam was not deceived, but the woman was deceived and became a transgressor. Yet woman will be saved through bearing children, if she continues in faith and love and holiness, with modesty (1 Tim 2:11–15).[6]

Finally, both Augustine and Aquinas held that, while marriage served as a legitimate outlet for sexual desire, it was still always at least a venial sin to seek sex, even in marriage, for any other aim than to have children.[7] This overtly double message about the goodness and legitimacy of sex was to work in a special way against women's sexuality in the modern period. It was brought into line with the view that the feminine attitude toward sex should be one of martyrlike tolerance and acquiescence, not one of desire, pleasure, or even active seeking of sexual expression as a form of intimate union with one's spouse. According to Rosemary Ruether:

> Whereas classical Christianity unhesitatingly saw women as less religious, spiritual, and moral than men, nineteenth-century culture typically saw women as inherently more moral, spiritual, and religious than men. Whereas earlier culture had regarded women as more sex-

ual than men, almost insatiably so, Victorian womanhood was regarded as almost asexual. The 'true woman' is almost incapable of feeling sexuality, and sexual desire is banished from her mind. Carnality is ceded to the male nature, as part of his rough dealings with the 'real world' of materialism and power.[8]

On the other hand, to give Aquinas credit with respect to his influence on later tradition, his own theory about sexuality was luckily not consistent. In other words, although he in some respects reflected a patriarchal mentality, he also was not entirely unable to consider women in their own right, or at least as more equal partners with men than his contemporaries would generally have allowed. Although, following Augustine, he saw women as the weaker sex and thought sex was only justified fully by procreation, he disagreed with Augustine that there is something intrinsically objectionable about sexual passion, and affirmed that sexual desire directed to the right purpose (childbearing) is good.[9] He also had a budding awareness that the real relation between men and women should be one of friendship and that, in marriage, sexual intercourse intensifies that friendship, as well as functioning to produce offspring.[10] Here we have the seeds of the view, only in the modern period to emerge after the full humanity and dignity of women began to gain recognition, that an equal partnership of spouses in marriage is possible, and that it extends further than the sexual cooperation necessary to produce the family.

The Catholic Christian tradition has, in fact, recently given a high profile to the affective dimensions of sex (intimacy and love), a level on which women and men are described as equal partners. As we shall see, however, even on this level of affective union, the tradition continues to communicate a hidden sexism, for the practical and social conditions of the sexual union—ostensibly of "equals"—continue to be defined in patriarchal terms. To be specific, John Paul II ascribes the primary significance of sex to the communion of persons which it enables and expresses, but continues to define the highest role of women as motherhood, while fatherhood is of relatively less importance for men.

3.
BIBLICAL SOURCES OF ETHICS

A chronically underutilized source of the Catholic ethical tradition is the scriptures. It is to the Bible that feminists have often turned in order to mount a critique of strands in the tradition which denigrate sex, patronize and even disparage women, and at the same time define women's role in almost entirely sexual-maternal terms. One example of recent rethinking of biblical materials is the contribution made to this lecture series in 1986 by Sandra M. Schneiders, *Women and the Word.*[11]

The scriptures have historically played a secondary role to natural law in Catholic theology and ethics. Often in the past biblical texts were used merely to confirm natural law conclusions. Since both Bible and "the natural" are necessarily read from the interpreter's particular cultural standpoint, we can see that both sources could readily be used to lend support to prevailing cultural views of women's inferiority. Standing within a history and a culture is an irreducible aspect of all human knowing, and Catholic ethics cannot be faulted because it, too, exhibits this limitation of perspective. The key point, however, is that moral viewpoints need constantly to be brought into dialogue with contemporary experience, with different nuances of the biblical tradition and its interpretations, and with voices or themes in the tradition which have not been adequately heard.

As far as the biblical literature is concerned, feminist thought increases the light on the fact that the scriptures contain not only patriarchal traditions defining women's sexuality in terms of kinship, marriage and childbearing, but also in relation to love, intimacy, and partnership (Song of Songs and Genesis 2). Although a text like 1 Timothy, or the *haustafeln* ("household codes"), commend submissiveness to women (e.g., Eph 5:22–24), Paul also speaks of gender equality in Christ (Gal 3:28), and depended in his ministry on many female leaders in the local churches (e.g., Prisca, in Rom 16:3–5). Hence, as we shall see, there is diversity in the biblical views of women and sexuality, especially as far as sex-based gender roles are concerned.

In presenting biblical resources for a view of women and sexuality, I want to focus not only on content but on *interpretative models*. That is to say, in addition to material which specifically addresses sex and gender, we find in the Bible itself some guidance for how to interpret authoritative writings and teachings. The basic interpretative model the Bible offers is a historical, communal, and developmental one. The Bible itself does not use "authorities," such as the teachings of Jesus, to assert a timeless, rigid, or legalistic basis for moral behavior. It presents them as original illustrations of covenant fidelity or discipleship which set a direction for future thought and practice without determining the latter in every detail. Authority does not preclude creativity, but evokes ongoing historical responses

16

which define the appropriate shape of communal life and individual conduct.

The Hebrew Scriptures

Before turning to the question of hermeneutical models, we shall first recall the biblical pictures of sexuality and of women's roles, beginning with the Hebrew scriptures (Old Testament). From a modern point of view not all pictures of women's sexuality and social roles are liberating. The social organization of ancient Israel was male, and most central figures in the Hebrew scriptures are male. Moreover, sexuality was extremely important in defining social roles within the community. The Israelite religion was one which was handed down from patriarchs to their sons, primarily through cultic practice and the repetition of an oral tradition on festal and ritual occasions.

An early harvest liturgy captures this religious reality, even as it also demonstrates that religious identity, and indeed the survival of the kinship line and of the covenant community, depends on male lines of descent. Set in the time just prior to the Israelites' entry into the Promised Land (Canaan) after their escape from Egypt, the words of the liturgy are framed as Moses' final instructions to the people. When the fruits of the harvest are about to be brought as a seasonal offering, the farmer is instructed to say to the priest, "I declare this day to the Lord your God that I have come into the land which the Lord swore to our fathers to give us." After the harvest offering has been set before the altar by the priest, the farmer is to announce, "A wandering Aramean [Jacob] is my father; and he went down into Egypt and sojourned there, few in number; and there he became a nation, great, mighty, and populous" (Dt 26:5). But after the Egyptians had treated the Hebrews "harshly," the Lord saw them, pitied them, and brought them to the land for which thanks is now being given (Dt 26:6–9). Those who repeat the liturgical tradition are even "today" joined with their ancestors as beneficiaries of God's saving deeds, as faithful, and as united in community. The continuity of historical community and of creedal confession depends on the male lineage.

A similar reflection of the importance of male continuity as the bearer of religious tradition occurs in the Exodus story itself, at the points where explanations of the feast of unleavened bread and of the custom of sacrificing to God the firstborn of the flocks occur. In the first case, the instruction is, "And you shall tell your son on that day, 'It is because of what the Lord did for me when I came out of Egypt' " (Ex 13:8). Similarly, the animal offerings are made because the Lord killed the firstborn sons and animals of the Egyptians and spared the Hebrew firstborn. The people are told, "when in time to come your son asks you, 'What does this mean?'," the male children shall be instructed in the faith they are to carry on from their fathers by learning that current practice is done for gratitude to God for having saved the ancestors, establishing a covenant with the people unto this day (Ex 13:14).

The importance of women in such a culture obviously resides in their maternal role. A woman with many children was blessed, particularly if her offspring numbered several sons, for they ensured her significance in family and cult. The subordination of women within the sexual order was due largely to the strong family ethos, with procreation as its center. "Within Israel procreation was particularly valued insofar as large Israelite families were considered to be the fulfillment of the promise made to Abraham."[12] Sexuality in general is treated matter-of-factly in the Hebrew scriptures, and is envisioned as part of the goodness of creation, especially because it provides for the increase of family, tribe, and nation. Male interest in controlling women amounted to control of their reproductive capacity to ensure purity of lineage and, hence, protection of the family assets by inheritance within the bloodline. Raymond Collins sums up the situation when he observes:

> A woman's husband was the *baal* (Gen 18:12), i.e., possessor or Lord; she was the *be'ulat ba'al* (Dt 22:22), i.e., that which is possessed. The language of the day, 'to marry' for the male, and 'to be given in marriage' for the female bespeaks the woman's social inferiority. . . . Only as a mother was a woman properly appreciated; thus the barren woman would mourn her infertility (Gen 30:1; Jg 11:37) or pray that the Lord take away her shame (1 Sm 1:10–11).[13]

The barren woman was cursed. What meaning could there be in her life? What role could she fill of importance to spouse, family, or community? A striking illustration, evocative in this era of the surrogate

19

mother, is found in the relation, born of desperation, between Sara and Hagar. When Sara, the wife of the original patriarch, Abraham, was getting on in years and had borne no children, she arranged for her maid, Hagar, to become a concubine for Sara's own husband. According to ancient custom, such an arrangement would enable Sara to claim any child of Hagar as her own, thus restoring her status in the religious and kinship community. Not only is Sara's own worth defined in terms of her procreative success, but also Hagar is valued only for her procreative contribution to the marriage of another woman. Her sexuality is used as a means to resolve another couple's genealogical difficulties. Even before the birth of Sara's child Ishmael, however, the arrangement turns sour, with Hagar holding Sara in "contempt," Sara treating Hagar "harshly," and the latter fleeing into the desert pending the protection of the Lord (Gen 16).

Only a few chapters later in the book of Genesis (18:20–19:29), we find a vastly more appalling example of the consequences of viewing women only in terms of their sexuality in a patriarchal culture. After the Lord has threatened to destroy the city of Sodom for its sinfulness, Abraham pleads with God to spare it if only ten just men can there be found. God agrees, and sends two angels on an investigative mission. They are received and hosted by Lot, whom the narrative presents as a holy man, and who is eventually indeed saved. During the visit, however, the men of Sodom gather about Lot's house, demanding that the visitors be sent out so that the native men can commit homosexual rape on them. The historical setting renders the act an outrage not only as an instance of sexual violence, but also because it would have amounted to a vile betrayal of the duty of hospitality, without which travelers could not even have survived in the deserts of the ancient Near East. Lot's proposed resolution of the affront is a frightening revelation of the dark side of a male piety only too ready to identify women's social and religious status in terms of the worth of their sexuality to fathers and husbands. Says Lot:

> I beg you, my brothers, do not act so wickedly. Behold, I have two daughters who have not known man; let me bring them out to you, and do to them as you please; only do nothing to these men, for they have come under the shelter of my roof (Gen 19:8).

Lot was willing to sacrifice his two daughters as an offering to the assailants, and proferred them with the encouragement that they were virgins. To have raped them would apparently have fallen significantly short of the "wickedness" about to be perpetrated on the pair of male visitors. A parallel incident occurs in Judges 19, where the victim is a concubine, raped all night and then abandoned dead or dying on her master's doorstep. With immense good cause Phyllis Trible entitles a book in which she confronts several such incidents in the Bible *Texts of Terror*.[14]

The extremity of these narrative examples is set against a culture which, historically, reinforced male supremacy in a usually less violent but pervasive manner. Until about the time of the monarchy, in the tenth century B.C., polygamous marriage still occurred in Israel (Gen 29:21–30; 2 Sam 5:13–16; 1 Kings 11:1, 3). As we have seen, concubinage also existed in order to promote the increase of male heirs, and to ensure that every male's lineage would be given adequate opportunity to survive. The same purpose was served by levirate marriage (Gen 38:8; Dt 25:5–10), though it also provided support for widows. Monogamy may have been an ideal: the book of Malachi advises, "let none be faithless to the wife of his youth. For I hate divorce, says the Lord the God of Israel . . ." (Mal 2:15–16). In reality, however, divorce was certainly a male prerogative, against which the wife had little recourse. The reason given for her severance did not necessarily have to meet any particularly stringent standard. The prescriptions for social living which follow the Decalogue in the book of Deuteronomy describe as within the law the situation in which "a man takes a wife and marries her," after which "she finds no favor in his eyes because he has found some indecency in her." In such a case he is obligated to write her a "bill of divorce" (freeing her to remarry). He is then able to effect the divorce if he merely "puts it [the bill] in her hand and sends her out of his house . . ." (Dt 24:1–4).

Not only was divorce not a choice open to women, but sex outside of marriage was prohibited much more stringently for them than for men as well. A young woman found to be not a virgin upon marriage would be stoned to death, for "playing the harlot in her father's house," i.e., disgracing the man who had control

22

of her (Dt 22:20–21). Both the man and woman will be stoned to death if a man either "lies with" the wife of another man or with a "betrothed virgin"—in both cases, the man has offended the property rights of another male, the husband or the bridegroom (Dt 22:22–24).

In the case of rape, a betrothed virgin's life will be spared, provided that the crime occurred in "the open country," where she could demonstrably not have called for help (Dt 22:25). In what today might seem an even greater affront to women's sexuality than the death penalty for fornication, a raped virgin who was *un*betrothed would be forcibly married off to the rapist. As "damaged goods," she would have become impossible for her father to match with any other prospect willing to pay the bride price, so the rapist is obliged to take her, without possibility of divorce, after giving the father "fifty shekels of silver" (Dt 28:29).

A man's use of a prostitute, however, was not punishable by law, whether he be married or not. Prostitutes, apparently, were women who had fallen through the fairly wide and numerous cracks in the social network of economic support for women. (What was the fate of women who did not find new husbands after having been given a bill of divorce, and whose families were unwilling or unable to receive them?) Since no men had any economic interest in "harlots," no real offense was committed either by them or their partners by their trade in their one remaining economic asset, their sexuality. Men were warned against resorting to the prostitute, lest they be seduced into a wanton life-style, but the question of the woman's welfare did not enter the moral picture (Prov 5; 7:5, 22–27).

Homosexual acts were forbidden for men in relation to cultic purity (Lev 18:22; 20:13), and bestiality was punishable by death for both men and women (Ex 22:19; Lev 18:23, 20:15–16). Also prohibited were incest, nakedness, and sexual intercourse during menstruation (Lev 20:11–12, 14, 17–21).

SOURCES OF RENEWAL

Despite the virtual equation of the identity of women with their sexuality as an instrument of procreation, there are some countervailing texts, themes, and figures in the Old Testament. Several prominent women, some of them associated with male heroes, managed to leave a mark in their own right, e.g., Sarah, Zipporah, Rebekah, Rachel, Leah, Deborah, Naomi, Ruth, Abigail, and Judith. (Also see Prov 31:3–31, on the good wife who manages a household). The Song of Solomon, traditionally often interpreted in spiritualized terms to refer to the union of God and soul or Christ and church, is actually a celebration of human love and sexual yearning, replete with sexual imagery. No religious references are contained directly within the text. There is no invocation of procreation or the kinship-based institution of marriage to justify sexuality, although the speakers are addressed, perhaps metaphorically, as "bride" and "bridegroom." The opening verses pour out the woman's longing for her lover:

O that you would kiss me with the
    kisses of your mouth!
For your love is better than wine . . . (1:2).

And her partner responds:

You have ravished my heart, my
    sister, my bride,
  you have ravished my heart with
    a glance of your eyes,
  with one jewel of your necklace.
How sweet is your love, my sister,
    my bride!
  how much better is your love than
    wine . . . (4:9–10).

This love poem portrays sexuality for both women and men as equal and passionate, an opportunity to express intimacy, exhilaration, and joy.

An even more fertile ground for feminist scholars wishing to reap a harvest of revised roles for women, are the creation stories in Genesis.[15] The passage from 1 Timothy cited above is not atypical of traditional interpretations of the creation of the first human creatures. The first creation of "Adam" and the derivation of a female companion from Adam's rib in Genesis 2 have been taken as signs of her inferiority, while the claim that she sinned first and led her husband into sin has been used to urge her submission. God's proclamation after the fall, in Genesis 3, your husband "shall rule over you" (3:16) has been taken as a divine mandate sealing women's destiny.

25

Feminist critics, closely reexamining the texts, challenge the validity of such interpretations. First, it may be noted, there are two different accounts of the creation. While they may be complementary, they should not be conflated. One consists in a rather brief affirmation that both the male and female were created in God's image and likeness (Gen 1:26–28). In this compact account, both male and female are evidently given dominion over the other animals, and are addressed with the blessing of increase, "Be fruitful and multiply . . ."

The second biblical creation narrative (Gen 2:4–25) is actually chronologically earlier, and takes the familiar form of an ancient myth of origin. Distinctive among other creation myths, however, the Hebrew story portrays the emergence of humankind not as a product of divine conflict, accident, or mistake, but as a deliberate creative enterprise, in which God fashions both male and female out of some preexisting matter, the dust of the earth and a rib, and blows into each the breath of life. Equal dignity belongs to each sex both because both are made in God's image (Gen 1) and because both are created through a personal and individual divine creative act (Gen 2:7, 22).

Moreover, the creation of the woman from the rib of the man signifies their commonality of nature, rather than the secondary nature of the woman. Prior to her creation, God had resolved, "It is not good that the man should be alone; I will make him a helper fit for him" (2:18). With an engaging, repetitive, folkloric touch, the narrator describes how God tries animal after animal, bringing them to the man in turn, and how the man names each, but with the end result that "there was not found a helper fit for him" (Gen 2:20). At this point, God takes a rib in order to succeed in making the man a suitable companion (the Hebrew word translated "helper" can also mean redeemer or savior, and does not carry the connotation that the person so described is a subordinate). Recognizing success when he sees it, the man exclaims,

> This at last is bone of my bones
> and flesh of my flesh . . . (Gen 2:23).

In a remarkable turn-about for what was historically the Hebrew practice of assimilating the wife to her husband's people, the narrator continues, "Therefore a man leaves his father and his mother and cleaves to his wife, and they become one flesh" (Gen 2:24).

This story reveals the sexual "one flesh" unity of man and woman as the immediate meaning of sexual differentiation. But while the story associates both woman and man as companions and partners in the task "to till and keep" the garden of Eden (Gen 2:15), it mentions neither the institution of marriage, nor parenthood as the meaning of sexuality or the determinant of gender roles. And, as we have seen, the mission of parenthood is charged to two partners, stamped equally with the divine likeness, in Genesis 1. In summary, the Genesis creation stories yield two narrative affirmations of equality of the sexes, and their sharing in the characteristically human tasks. Only one of these texts mentions procreation in connection with sexual differentiation, and the second text envisions "one flesh" union as an expression of the unity in nature of the woman and the man.

The idyllic picture changes in Genesis 3. Designed as a symbolic representation of the inexplicable fascination and persuasiveness of evil, if not actually of its origin, the story of the fall introduces for the first time the gender role allocations and hierarchies that are the mark of sin. Actively dialoguing with the serpent, and all too easily convinced by him, the woman takes the forbidden fruit and eats (Gen 3:1–7). The man, a passive and, judging from the story, an unreflective character, accepts unquestioningly the fruit from his mate, and eats it also.

Hearing the approach of God, they hide in shame of their disobedience. And, accused by God, they shift the blame. The moral of the story, however, is that active leadership in sin and passive acquiescence in sin bring equal guilt. God outlines for the pair their dismal future, and does so in terms of an ironic reversal of roles. To the woman, active sinner, God portrays a passive suffering—the pain of childbirth—as well as her husband's "rule" over her (Gen 3:16). To the man, passive sinner who readily but wrongfully consumed the appealing fruit of nature, God portrays an active struggle against the earth, now turned miserly in its provision of human sustenance.

> [C]ursed is the ground because of you;
>   in toil you shall eat of it all the
>   days of your life;
> . . . In the sweat of your face

> you shall eat bread
> till you return to the ground . . . (Gen 3:17, 19).

The judgments of God do not necessarily reveal the divine will for humanity's indefinite future. What they surely do reveal are the distorting effects of sin on the creation, at the personal, social, and even cosmic levels. Sexual hierarchy, separation of roles, and suffering hardly capture the design of creation; it is only after humanity's willful fall from its created harmony that male-female partnership is transformed into strife and pain. The distortion of human sexuality and of its social mediation via gender roles is the result of sin. When considered in relation to the patriarchal traditions undergirding the rest of the biblical literature, the Genesis creation stories stand out as a utopian ideal, an ideal which no doubt functioned as a critical standard over against the social realities of Israelite society at the time the texts were composed, and which can so function in feminist biblical interpretation today. Similarly, the Song of Songs lifts up, however briefly, an emotional and affective dimension of sexuality which would have otherwise been rarely affirmed in the procreative marital ethos of most ancient cultures.

Scripture scholar Pheme Perkins notes that the complex dynamic of sexism and egalitarian critique in the Old Testament goes beyond a combination of internally contradictory voices which challenge the reader to make decisions about relative worth. Pointing out that the book of Jubilees explicitly "corrects" some of the patriarchal and even "terrorizing" plots in Genesis and Judges, she demonstrates that within the biblical canon itself there is a pattern of revision of "authoritative" texts, which brings into a different configuration elements of their message which later communities recognized as unjust and even irreligious in relation to the righteousness and compassion of God. For instance, Jubilees changes the story of Sarah and Hagar so as to rectify the former's abuse of the latter. Other stories whose details are changed in a direction less oppressive to female victims involve Judah and Tamar, Bilhah and Dinah. Observes Perkins, "Some of the overtones which a feminist approach from the perspective of the battered and abused women amplifies could be heard in the second-century B.C."[16]

New Testament

Diversity in approaches to sexuality, especially women's sexuality, can also be found in the New Testament. However, it is clear that the ministry of Jesus does set female-male relations on a radically different plane. Many exegetes have commented on the critical function of Jesus' treatment of women in relation to his culture. If one word could be found to describe the socially transformative effect of the kingdom Jesus preached, a good candidate would be "inclusiveness" or "solidarity." By associating with and accepting hospitality from the social outcasts of his day and the marginalized classes, Jesus, in very concrete and socially threatening ways, broke down traditional boundaries of exclusion and of domination, of dependency and of power.[17]

> Jesus seeks to establish new patterns of personal relationship and human solidarity among the people of his world that represent liberation and healing for their hunger, their indebtedness, their violence toward one another, their neglected parents, their widows, their women at the margins of society.[18]

The most fundamental reason for woman's release from an all-inclusive identity as wife and mother in the New Testament and in early Christianity is the shift in the nature of the religious community itself. No longer is the faith passed on generationally, via transmission of traditions from fathers to sons. With its imminent eschatology, its expectation that God would soon bring history to a climax and judge both nations and individual lives, early Christianity—beginning with Jesus—spread the "good news" by preaching repentance and conversion (Mark 1:15). The Christian disciple was not one who was born into the family of faith, but one who heard the word of Jesus and was transformed by new kingdom life.

A striking example is found in the synoptic gospels, in passages in which Jesus specifically turns away any suggestion that Mary, as his biological mother, should have a special claim on his attention or role in his ministry (Mk 10:29–30; Mt 10:37; Lk 14:26). Luke's gospel best illustrates the alternative definition of discipleship that Jesus put forth, and which could include his biological relatives on a different basis. While Jesus is preaching,

> . . . his mother and his brothers came to him, but they could not reach him for the crowd. And he was told, 'Your mother and your brothers are standing outside, desiring to see you.' But he said to them, 'My mother and my brothers are those who hear the word of God and do it' (Lk 8:19–21).

Another popular and even more radical image in feminist biblical interpretation is provided by characterizing Mary Magdalene as an apostle. Mary Magdalene has long been misinterpreted in Christian history as a sinner and a prostitute, neither of which designations are borne out by the biblical identification of Mary simply as a woman out of whom "seven demons" were cast (Lk 8:2). She stands as an example of the historical tendency to identify women's vice and virtue in exclusively sexual terms. If we go to the biblical traditions, however, we see that all four gospels recognize Mary Magdalene as the first witness to the resurrection of Jesus.

In John's gospel, she meets the Pauline criteria of apostleship. As she stands weeping by the tomb on Easter morning, Jesus appears to her, and commissions her to return to the other disciples and report upon his presence and his words (Jn 20:11–18). Paul himself, of course, was not a follower of Jesus during Jesus' lifetime, and in fact was a persecutor of the early Christian movement. However, he claims to have been converted by a vision of Jesus and to have received a mandate from Jesus to preach the gospel, in light of which he, too, serves in the role of "apostle" (cf. 1 Cor 9:1–2, 15:5–11; Gal 1:11–16). The New Testament definition of apostle is not necessarily limited to "the twelve" who accompanied Jesus during his ministry. If apostleship can be expanded to include Paul and even Mary Magdalene, then modern roles supposedly derived from it are not obviously limited to definitions based upon the identity of the original dozen.

Jesus interacted with many faithful women during his lifetime, such as Mary of Bethany and her sister Martha, Joanna, Susanna, and the women mentioned in Luke's gospel who traveled with Jesus and supported him by their own means (Lk 8:3). Never does Jesus treat women as though their worth were to be defined in terms of typical gender expectations. It is striking that sexuality plays a relatively small role in the New Testament at all. Only twice does Jesus direct his concern directly toward it, and in both cases he protects women from the customs of his day and culture. When confronted with the stoning of a woman discovered in the act of adultery, he interferes with the death by stoning to which Jewish law had consigned her (John 8:1–11). Without approving her sexual infidelity, Jesus refuses to condemn her, and sends her to renew her life. Jesus is also portrayed as resisting the custom of (male-initiated) divorce, even appealing to the "one flesh" union of the creation (Mt 19:3–9), and holding the first husband responsible for the "adultery" of the remarried wife who has been sent away by him (Mt 5:31–32).

Yet considered on the whole, even the New Testament provides us with an ambiguous picture of women's roles and the significance of their sexuality. The ambivalence of early Christianity toward the iconoclastic attitudes of Jesus is well evidenced when the earlier Pauline epistles are compared to the "pastoral" epistles, the later letters which were written in Paul's name to address new or continuing issues as the first Christian communities entered their second generation of existence.

A certain egalitarian impetus in Paul's own thinking is captured in the baptismal formula of Galatians 3:28: "There is neither Jew nor Greek, there is neither slave nor free, there is neither male nor female; for you are all one in Christ Jesus." Of course, this ideal for Christian community does not necessarily describe actual conditions in the first century. However, it is also clear that there were many women active in leadership in Paul's own churches. These include Chloe, a leader in Corinth; Prisca, who with her husband, Aquila, hosted a church in their home; Phoebe, a deaconess of the church in Cenchreae; and a probable Junia (not "Junianus," as the translation often goes), mentioned by Paul as "outstanding among the apostles" (Rom 16:7).[19]

At the same time, Paul to an extent, and certainly those writing later in the Pauline school of thought, reflected their culture's expectation that women in general would follow the leadership of men. I Timothy 8 is a clear example. Also to be contended with are the *haustafeln*, commonly repeated in antiquity to prescribe properly ordered relationships among household members,

34

under the authority of the paterfamilias. These codes have been incorporated in the New Testament. A representative case is Colossians 3:18–4:1. In part, this passage commands, "Wives, be subject to your husbands, as is fitting in the Lord. Husbands, love your wives, and do not be harsh with them," and contains similar instructions for fathers and children, masters and slaves. A parallel, Ephesians 5:21–28, a text often used in Catholicism precisely to define Christian marriage as sacramental, compares husbands to Christ and wives to the church, in exhorting wives to be "subject in everything" to their husbands.

Even in an authentically Pauline letter, 1 Corinthians, which contains the most material on sexuality in the New Testament, we receive mixed messages. On the one hand, Paul seems to see woman and man as equal sexual partners when he counsels against celibate marriages, saying that spouses should give to one another their conjugal rights, and that neither husband nor wife "rule over" their own body, but the spouse does (1 Cor 7:3–4). At the same time, Paul expresses a general preference for celibacy in a life without marriage, so that one can be free to fix one's total attention on "the Lord" and the coming of the kingdom (1 Cor 7:35). He also advises widows not to remarry, though he does not formulate this as a command (1 Cor 7:39–40).

Later in the same letter, Paul seems to work on the assumption that women will be active in public prayer and prophecy, though for the sake of good order in the community, he instructs women taking such roles to respect current notions of public decency by keeping their hair bound up and their heads perhaps covered (1 Cor 11:2–16).[20] However, only three chapters later, Paul appears to betray his own assumptions:

> As in all the churches of the saints, the women should keep silence in the churches. For they are not permitted to speak, but should be subordinate, as even the law says. If there is anything they desire to know, let them ask their husbands at home. For it is shameful for a woman to speak in church (1 Cor 14:23b–35).

The opening argument about established church practice suggests a date for this passage later than 53–54 A.D., the date of 1 Corinthians, only twenty years after the death of Jesus, and during the period of the first missionary endeavors. Hence, some scholars suggest that this passage, and perhaps even 1 Corinthians 11, is an interpolation, an insertion reflecting later church concerns about male and female roles in family and society.[21]

Elisabeth Schüssler Fiorenza, in her widely noted work, *In Memory of Her,* argues that subordinationist texts, especially the *haustafeln,* reflect an attempt of the second-century churches to reach a compromise with the larger Greco-Roman society which threatened them with exclusion and even extermination. The early movement built around Jesus had taken the form of an inclusive and egalitarian discipleship community, but that very equality made for subversive effects on the enveloping social fabric, a danger that the culture was not slow to recognize.[22]

SEEKING INTERPRETIVE MODELS

Whether or not subordinationist material dates from the period of Jesus' ministry or from the next generation, or is original Pauline material versus an interpolation, the interpreter approaching the Bible, especially the feminist interpreter, needs to determine its normative status for Christian faith and practice. Schüssler Fiorenza herself is as blunt as she is radical. First of all, all theology, and that includes the theologies of the biblical authors, represents an advocacy stance, and has political implications. In other words, no theological position is "neutral," "objective," or "unbiased." All theological expressions come out of historical contexts and political commitments. Liberation theology, of which feminist theology is a version, casts its lot with the struggle for liberation of oppressed peoples, including women. Thus, the authoritative text is the liberative text, judged from the standpoint of women's experience.[23]

> A feminist theological interpretation of the Bible that has as its canon the liberation of women from oppressive sexist structures, institutions, and internalized values must, therefore, maintain that only the nonsexist and non-androcentric traditions of the Bible and

the nonoppressive traditions of biblical interpretation have the theological authority of revelation if the Bible is not to continue as a tool
for the oppression of women.[24]

Schüssler Fiorenza recommends a "hermeneutics of sus-
picion" rather than a "hermeneutics of consent" in approaching the canon, and is willing to accept the conse-
quence that not all the materials usually considered to
be "revelation" for the Christian churches can be help-
ful or even usable in constructing a feminist theology
and an egalitarian Christian community.

Other authors, interested in a feminist critique of
traditional religious views of sex and gender, work toward a hermeneutics lying somewhere between suspi-
cion and consent. In other words, they take up a critical
agenda toward religiously-based patriarchy, adopting a
stance more like "reconstruction" of oppressive texts, a
stance in which experientially and theologically unacceptable meanings are not denied, but in which such
texts are examined for the possibility of other aspects or
layers of meaning which still might function positively
within a renewed theology.

For instance, one might see the *haustafeln* as unacceptable for their compromise with the prevailing social
ethos of domination, realized across all levels of human
relationships, both familial and public. At the same
time, these texts represent positively the recognition
that Christianity cannot be sectarian, nor avoid human
injustice by withdrawing entirely from the larger social
world. Indeed, it would be impossible for Christians
completely to exempt themselves from "entanglement"

in the beliefs, values and institutions of their social place and time. This is precisely what is meant by saying that Christianity is a "historical" religion, and even that all theology has to assume an advocacy stance "for or against" the social arrangements it confronts.

The contribution of the *haustafeln* is that they stand as an example of engagement with an unjust surrounding culture and an attempt (however inadequate) to transform it. Christian community is embodied in the cultural forms available, but it should also challenge and transform those very same expectations and structures. While the household codes of pagan antiquity merely reinforced submission to dominance, the Christian transcriptions of those patterns made an effort to transform familial oppressions: husbands, fathers, and masters were instructed in forbearance and "love" toward those who were subject to them. In retrospect, we can appreciate that these transformations did not go far enough. A broader and much deeper challenge to the institutions of patriarchy and slavery was needed. The "message" of the text is not to replicate the family relationships it envisioned in the first century, but to constantly challenge family forms (and other social institutions) which are oppressive.

Schüssler Fiorenza offers an image of the development of the biblical traditions, and the communities they reflect, which comes close to coherence with the above reconstructive model. Provocatively, she recommends that the appropriate paradigm for biblical revelation would not define the New Testament as an "archetype" of all adequate realizations of discipleship, but as a historical "prototype." Both are "original models," but "an archetype is an ideal form that establishes an unchanging timeless pattern, whereas a prototype is not a binding timeless pattern or principle."[25] In other words, a prototype is something like a first run, a historical experiment which may be improved upon in the future. Later versions will bear a recognizable similarity to the original, but will not infallibly replicate any particular set of essential features as though cast from exactly the same mold.

Perhaps it would be possible for a feminist theology and ethics of sex and gender to maintain its critical edge, while still adopting a *prima facie* positive attitude toward the liberating potential of the canon. Otherwise, why do "liberationist" or "feminist" theology *as Christian theology* at all? Working out of the Mennonite tradition, Willard Swartley also has taken up the paradigmatically perplexing biblical questions of *Slavery, Sabbath, War and Women.*[26] Like Schüssler Fiorenza, he approaches biblical texts from an appreciation of their diversity, of the ways in which "the Bible" has been used simplistically to justify opposite moral positions in history, and out of a conviction that many of these so-called "biblical" moral positions are indefensible on the basis of Christian and human experience. However, at face value, his agenda as an interpreter contrasts with that of Schüssler Fiorenza. Swartley is evidently committed to retrieving and reconciling as much of the canon as possible, and especially to permitting "unacceptable" biblical texts to challenge modern-day presuppositions.

Yet, at the same time, Swartley is cognizant of the

historical nature of interpretation, and admits that the Bible can only *have* authority in the community for which it *is* an authority. In other words, the Bible is constantly subjected to the experiential criterion of the community whose identity is formed by its transmission of biblical texts and traditions. Affirming that, "[i]n biblical revelation God acts and speaks within history, within the limits of a people's experience," Swartley affirms that "biblical authority requires an understanding of divine revelation as dynamically interacting with history and culture. . . ."[27] Cultural patterns are to be recognized and even adopted by Christianity, *insofar as* they are consistent with the gospel.[28]

Swartley expresses the interaction of Christianity and culture by means of a "missionary principle." This principle is meant to reflect the development of the gospels and epistles themselves through a process of carrying the good news of Jesus' life, death, and resurrection into foreign cultures in which the originally Jewish terms of the faith were not always effective or even comprehensible. Just as the first Christians articulated their faith in vital interaction with other religions, philosophies, and cultures, so Christianity today both speaks to and is informed by the settings in which it lives, grows, and changes.

> In taking the differences in history and culture seriously, biblical revelation engages in a two-way contextualization: contextualizing the gospel to people in their world and culture and at the same time contextualizing the varied cul-

41

tures and experiences of people into confor-
mity with God's will and kingdom. . . .[29]

In summary, *experience,* e.g., of the liberation of
women, is a criterion of the revelatory meaning of the
Bible. In fact, as the contemporary interpreter's awareness grows of the historical, contextual, and perspecti-
val nature of all knowledge, one might even say that the
hermeneutical situation is captured better if we see the
Bible as meaningful only *within* historical experiences.
"Experience" is hardly an independent standard which
is brought "to" the Bible, as though the latter had significance "in itself" apart from the ongoing and formative
struggle of the community of faith with the biblical texts
and traditions.

As Letty Russell has formulated it, the emerging
feminist paradigm of biblical and theological truth
claims centers on *authority as partnership,* a view in which
"reality is interpreted in the form of a circle of interdependence," in which participants are presented with "a
common task of creating an interdependent community
of humanity and nature."[30] Russell specifically directs
her remarks to hierarchical assumptions about authority invested in persons or groups in ecclesial communities. However, the model applies equally well to the relation among the various sources of authority to which
persons and groups may appeal. For instance, faithful
but critical *experience* and the normativity of *scripture* are
interdependent and mutually informing poles of one
historical and communal reality—pluriform and chang-
ing, but not without identity and consistency. The other
side of the coin, then, is that the Bible also confronts

and may reshape our perceptions of ourselves, our communities, our faith, and our moral relationships. Indeed, as Schüssler Fiorenza, Swartley, and others illustrate, it is the emergence to Christian consciousness of the egalitarian aspects of the biblical collection that allows a successful critique of the patriarchy that the same materials have been used to justify. As we move toward a more feminist Christian appreciation of women's sexuality and its relation to gender assumptions, we can also draw on biblical and Christian traditions to challenge aspects of the contemporary Western "experience" of sexuality in which we share as members of our culture.

Finally, we may nuance our vision of the interdependence of mutually critical sources in Christian community, practice, and theology by noting that scripture and experience are complemented by further reference points, such as tradition, theology, and church teachings; philosophy; and the social and natural sciences which describe human experience with methods which allow systematic generalizations intended to include multiple individuals and groups.[31] All of these resources have obvious importance for a moral understanding of sexuality.

A related and quite important issue that emerges once the complementarity of such sources has been established is that of their priority. Perhaps one has acknowledged that scripture neither provides a revealed moral code, nor is completely irrelevant to contemporary moral concerns. Instead, scripture offers a basic orientation for moral thinking and judgment. But if the possibility of mutual challenge among the sources (e.g., scripture and experience) has been acknowledged, then, as James Gustafson notes, the "principal problem is to determine how decisive the authority of scripture is for one's moral judgment."[32] This dilemma is allayed somewhat by recognizing that, after all, no one source among the many is adduced independently of the others. Nonetheless, if any critique is to be possible, as feminist theology and ethics certainly assume, then Gustafson's question cannot be entirely dismissed. Various authors and Christian communities have taken different approaches to an answer. While many feminists give ultimate authority to women's experience, other theologians finally put their confidence in biblical revelation. In either case, the honest interpreter has to recognize hermeneutical complexity and lack of closure on many issues, not least of all gender and sexuality.

4.
EXPERIENCE, SEXUALITY,
AND INTIMACY

The Roman Catholic tradition is particularly hospitable
to the assumption that investigation of human experience will contribute fruitfully to normative ethics. The
approach implied by the term "natural law" validates
the appropriateness of the experiential criterion in the
discovery of moral truth. Natural law morality is based
precisely on theories about human experience, theories
derived from basic and shared human realities, such as
life, sex, and society. In point of fact, an honest investigation of women's experience, especially in relation to
sex and gender, tends to prompt a reexamination of
some of the conclusions which natural law moral theology, as defined and practiced in the past, has drawn. But
just as the retrieval of liberating themes from the biblical literature is essentially an affirmation of the continuing worth of scripture in forming Christian identity and
morality; so the recovery of the feminine perspective on
the human is essentially an affirmation that Christian
ethics should continue to be informed by common human values experientially discovered.

The feminist theologian Rosemary Radford Ruether is never more Catholic than when she insists on "the full humanity of women" as the final court of appeal.[33] Along with the tradition which she often criticizes but never entirely abandons, she assumes that at some level it still makes sense to speak of a "common human nature," that this nature can be known and appreciated at least in its fundamental outlines by well-intentioned persons thinking rationally, and that it is possible to use agreement about what is best for human beings to begin to change sinful social structures. Her method and its presuppositions have much in common with Aquinas and with the modern papal social encyclicals, even though she uses the method against many of their specific conclusions.

As we look back over our consideration of the biblical resources for a feminist appreciation of sexuality, we will recall that patriarchal assumptions about the inferiority of women and their identity as childbearers have been undercut—even within the biblical literature—by the created equality of the first man and woman's "one flesh" union and their social partnership, as well as by the blessing of increase as directed to both sexes. In addition, the dominant procreative motif in understanding sexuality received a counterpoint in the Song of Songs, biblical poetry exalting the erotic and affective meanings of sex.

If we turn now to experiential explorations of the meaning of sexuality, we will discover a complement to this "subversive" minority voice in the biblical literature which testifies to the importance of sex as an expression of intimacy and love. In modern Western Christianity, experiential sources, especially in Catholicism, have also been utilized to join eroticism and psychological intimacy to the procreative significances of human sexuality. In fact, affective intimacy or "love" is the meaning which we are today most likely to lift up as primary to sexuality. Even in official Roman Catholic teaching (to be reviewed below), sexual intercourse, as a pleasurable and erotic experience, is appreciated for its power to communicate and enhance intimacy.

In the twentieth century, Freud's theories about the pervasive effect of sexuality on personality have made way for "a new understanding of sexuality as language for the newly discovered sacred, spiritual-carnal realm of the interpersonal."[34] As Margaret Farley suggests, "sexuality is an expression of something beyond itself. Its power is a power for union and its desire a desire for intimacy."[35] Theologians have gone further than Freud in connecting sex, not only with the deepest reserves of the personality, but with the heights of human communion, and even with the transcendent.

The language of sex *as* language has become an important way to express its unitive and communicative powers. In the 1960's the philosopher Paul Ricoeur described sex as a language which expresses tenderness.[36] The analogy of sex to language has been furthered by several subsequent thinkers, especially in the work of André Guindon, author of *The Sexual Language*.[37] Guindon emphasizes psychological theories of human sexual development, and concludes not only that sex has an intrinsic communicative character, but also that pleasure should have a positive role in the theological and moral interpretation of sex and of its potential as language. Other theologians have taken up the linguis-

47

tic metaphor as central to a revised meaning of sexuality, as is well demonstrated in Vincent Genovesi's introduction to a contemporary Catholic sexual ethics. Arguing that sex has two essential dimensions, the genital and the affective, Genovesi ties these together in the relational potential of sex. "Our sexuality is simply essential both to our becoming fully human and to our human becoming." Sex "symbolizes our call to communication and communion," and "encourages and facilitates our response to this invitation" through a concrete response.[38] Even more idealistically, John Dwyer sees sex as offering self-transcendence and "a liberation from egoism." "Sexual love awakens the feeling of wanting to give and wanting to please, of wanting to give of oneself wholly and entirely, without reserve and without calculation."[39]

Although the evolution of a positive and even celebratory appropriation of human sexuality as a good is a vast improvement over narrow, apprehensive, and almost cynical readings of sex as a dangerous necessity, redeemed only by procreation, Ricoeur himself cautioned that an overly lyrical mysticism about sex can also be dangerous. Sex can have—and not all that infrequently—manipulative and destructive manifestations. Sexuality "is not simple, and . . . the integration of its multiple components is an unending task." For instance, tenderness must be kept in balance with eroticism as the cultivation of pleasure. Ricoeur concludes that, at least in our culture, marriage may be the best opportunity for the nurturance of a sexual bond which is not only tender but durable; and that the future task of sexual ethics is to preserve the meaning of sex as both spiritual and physical.

Perhaps the best path to a theology and morality of sex which is integrated and even disciplined is to avoid taking sex and sexuality as such as the point of departure. Any focus on sex which separates it as an independent moral object or realm of philosophical scrutiny will likely fail to perceive one important aspect: sex is not an end in itself but an *expression* of human relationship.

RECENT ROMAN CATHOLIC TEACHING

Current Roman Catholic teaching on sexuality is characterized by the following four traits. 1) It aims at a new stress on the *interpersonal,* in addition to the procreative. 2) It attempts to set or reaffirm *norms* for sex, even while recognizing the importance of intimacy (as equal to or even more important than acts) in defining sexual morality. 3) At the most concrete and practical level, sexual norms are nonetheless derived within an essentially *patriarchal,* procreative model, especially regarding women's sexuality. 4) Even while affirming the personal and relational significances of sexuality, official teaching still elaborates norms for sexual behavior around a focus on specific sex *acts* (or specific procreative acts).

As recently as 1930, official papal teaching, in the form of the encyclical *Casti connubii,* affirmed that procreation is the purpose of sexual acts. Love or intimacy ("mutual and intimate harmony") was recognized as important—a shift not to be belittled. But this document still ranked procreation and mutual help as primary and secondary ends of sexual acts and of marriage also.[40] However, the Second Vatican Council set the stage for a breakthrough by mentioning as on an equal level "conjugal love" and "the responsible transmission of life."[41] The so-called birth control encyclical, *Humanae vitae* (Paul VI, 1968), published shortly after the council, disappointed expectations of those who had hoped that the personalist themes increasingly resounding even in these Vatican documents would override the old procreative focus and permit it to be subordinated to other marital and familial goods. But the encyclical stood firm on the impermissibility of contraception. At the same time, though, it affirms fairly straightforwardly that love and procreation are the "two great realities of married life"—inseparable but equal meanings of sex.[42] Although the document introduced this proposal in terms of "the moral teaching on marriage proposed with constant firmness by the teaching authority of the Church," the fact was that the church's tradition had undergone a quiet revolution.

Important factors in making this turn of events possible were a modern appreciation of the dignity of the individual and an emerging awareness of women's equality.[43] These themes had been given expression within Christian sexual ethics by continental theologians influenced by phenomenological philosophy.[44] The new trend which they initiated was to see sexuality primarily in the context of intersubjective union. Sex as an act of love enables and expresses the marital partnership, of which the fruit—not the primary purpose—is

50

the creation of a child. Personalist themes were quickly adopted in Catholic sexual ethics, and not only by critics of the ban on contraception. They inform papal teaching itself. *Casti connubii* is already an example.

The language of *Humanae vitae* is even more striking when it describes conjugal love as *total,* as "a very special form of personal friendship," in which spouses "generously share everything." "Whoever truly loves his marriage partner loves not only for what he receives, but for the partner's self, rejoicing that he can enrich his partner with the gift of himself."[45] Moreover, the encyclical addresses a duty, not of "procreation," but of "responsible parenthood." The intention to procreate is now, in principle, separable from sexual acts, as long as the biological structure of the act is preserved. Paul VI sees the love union of spouses as intrinsically and naturally fertile, and, invoking the "natural law," insists that "each and every marriage act must remain open to the transmission of life."[46] According to this viewpoint, a *true* act of love must meet a biological criterion: the integrity of the biological process which includes sexual intercourse and can under conditions of fertility lead to conception.[47] In the end, the personalist shift has been incomplete. Current teaching attaches conclusions once derived within the old biologistic, procreative, and hierarchical model of sexuality, and especially women's sexuality (as defined primarily in terms of motherhood, domesticity, and submission to the husband/father instead of equal partnership).

The writings of John Paul II continue on this conflicted course. On one level, he expresses a high appreciation for the interpersonal meanings of sex and the egalitarianism which should characterize sexual union, spousehood, parenthood, and even social roles. On the other hand, the human and moral meanings of sexuality remain tightly tied to biological conditions, and women find their true and natural fulfillment in a role derived from their sexuality: motherhood. In *Reflections on Humanae vitae,* the pope even adopts the "sex as language" metaphor to make his point. Sex is "the 'language of the body,' " which has "an important interpersonal meaning, especially in reciprocal relationships between man and woman."[48] But in this language, "the conjugal act 'signifies' not only love, but also potential fecundity, and therefore it cannot be deprived of its full and adequate significance by artificial means."[49] The pope also invests the sexual body with a "nuptial meaning," and interprets both the procreative mandate and the marital commitment into the Genesis creation stories, freely combining the first and second versions:

> Genesis 2:24 speaks of the finality of man's masculinity and femininity, in the life of the spouses-parents. Uniting with each other so closely as to become 'one flesh,' they will subject, in a way, their humanity to the blessing of fertility, namely, 'procreation,' of which the first narrative speaks (Gn 1:28).[50]

Naturally, one need not go far to realize that the humanity of the woman will be "subjected to fertility" much more than that of the man, although the creation narratives (as distinct from the depiction of sinful human relationships) in no way assign procreation more to her as a task, vocation, or fulfillment. Has the new language of intimacy simply been co-opted in favor of the old gender roles and the constraint of human sexual expression by its procreative potential and its physiological structures?

In *Familiaris Consortio* (the 1980 Apostolic Exhortation, *On the Family*), John Paul II celebrates parenthood as an expression of the love of woman and man, in language which almost duplicates that of the personalist revisionists of half a century before. "Fecundity is the fruit and sign of conjugal love, the living testimony of the full reciprocal self-giving of the spouses . . ."[51] At the same time, however, we are reminded that "the innate language that expresses the total reciprocal self-giving of husband and wife is overlaid, through contraception, by an objectively contradictory language, namely, that of not giving oneself totally to the other." Spouses resorting to artificial means of fulfilling their duty of responsible parenthood are accused of "a falsification of the inner truth of conjugal love, which is called upon to give itself in personal totality."[52] "Personal totality" is identified with conditions of the act of sexual intercourse as a merely physical reality.

The question of the actual social context in which these ideals of personal totality as unfettered fecundity is played out when, on the one hand, the pope asserts, quite admirably, that there "is no doubt that the equal dignity and responsibility of men and women fully justifies women's access to public functions," but adds immediately, "the true advancement of women requires that clear recognition be given to the value of their maternal and family role, by comparison with all other public roles and all other professions."[53] The centrality of motherhood in the papal view of women's identity is strikingly evident in his pastoral letter, *Mulieris Dignitatem.*[54] Even non-mothers (such as vowed celibate religious women) find their true identity and mission in callings which are analogous to motherhood. "Motherhood is linked to the personal structure of the woman . . ."[55] In a manner which should give pause to feminists who want to idealize women's special traits without very careful consideration of the limits to be placed on such a program, the pope almost foretells the wording of Sara Ruddick (see below). Motherhood gives women in general a special capacity ("predisposition") to pay "attention" to other persons, and even a special capacity for love.[56] Whatever the benign intentions and romantic appeal of this rhetoric of women's sexuality glorified as motherhood, I agree with the common sense of Margaret O'Brien Steinfels, who finds the magisterium's image of feminine "nurturing, maternal qualities" to be "strangely implausible," and "separated as by a chasm from the ordinary experience of an increasing number of women and men."[57]

WHAT THEN, IS THE HUMAN SEXUAL EXPERIENCE?

One book which is successful in making the point that an experiential renewal of natural law tradition will have to attend more concretely to sex as not only relational but as also developmental for each person and couple (and hence unavoidably ambiguous) is *A Sense of Sexuality* by Evelyn Eaton Whitehead and James D.

Whitehead.[58] The Whiteheads' study of sexuality, full of anecdote and description, is quite illustrative of an experiential approach, and as such reveals a Roman Catholic sensibility. James Whitehead is a pastoral theologian and Evelyn Whitehead is a developmental psychologist, disciplines which furnish them the standpoint and tools to arrive at a treatment of sexuality which is more practical than theoretical; and which is tolerant, realistic, and nuanced in its account of the ambiguous potential of human sexuality. This book puts intimacy first, and in fact demonstrates how intimacy characterizes a variety of important yet quite ordinary human relationships. Only then do the authors develop the possibility that some of these relationships will be appropriately expressed in specifically sexual intimacy. If sex is to retain its value as an expression of relationship, the sexual "act" will never supersede in importance that fundamental relational context, which is the very condition of the possibility of sex's *moral* significance. Because it is humanly expressive and relational—not just physical and reproductive—sexuality must be connected with the full moral life.

The failure to appreciate that relationships are key in defining personal identity, and in locating sexuality within identity, is well attested, not only in official church teaching, but also in many popular attitudes. The Whiteheads note the treatment usually given to the so-called "single" person. The term "single" is "a social classification rather than a self-description," meaning that it does not particularly correlate with the self-understanding of unmarried persons themselves. The quite superficial assignment of persons to this category is premised on the culturally validated assumption that marriage is the normal and normative human state. But, to the contrary, single persons usually understand *themselves,* not in relation to matrimony, but in relation to other roles which they fulfill. For instance, roles created by friendships, family, and vocational choices are certainly more central to the identity of the so-called "single" than the non-role of not sharing the marital bond which others may have chosen. (The anomaly of the "single" designation becomes apparent when I consider that I might identify myself as a mother or a teacher or even a wife, but not as an unfather, or an un-lawyer, or an unsingle.) A single woman may see herself as a woman, a Christian, a sister or daughter, a teacher or lawyer, a tennis or jogging partner, and so on. But if she sees "unmarried woman" as part of her core identity, it is at least in part because a set of social categories have marginalized the importance of her own experience of positive role-fulfillment even in her own self-understanding.

Intimacy and Friendship as Sexual Experiences

Turning to experience to renew our perspective on sexuality, we find confirmed that it is above all a *relational* capacity. This fact was recognized in older, patriarchal Christian models of sexual meaning in the fact that sex was located, by means of its procreative potential, in the networks of family, clan, and nation. Today, reflection on sexuality can complement sex's relational potential as *social* (procreative) by affirming its relational potential as *interpersonal* (intimate).

One of the most important categories of human and moral relation is friendship, as Aristotle saw—and as Aquinas began to see, it is even possible that sexuality can shape the expression of some friendships, finding through friendship its genuine moral worth. As the Whiteheads note, most friendships do not involve sexual forms of communication. But a sexual friendship shares with the other types the fact that "the partners become *reliable emotional confidants.*" A friendship implies not only emotional self-disclosure, but also trustworthiness—a mutual willingness to share and accept frailties.[59] This indicates that sex as intimacy also implies sex as commitment.

If we specifically consider *women's* accounts of the crucial dimensions of the experience of sexuality, we find that intimacy as trustworthy friendship assumes an especially high profile. Feminist theologians and ethicists characteristically establish the context of intimate friendship first, and only afterwards proceed to the question of sexual expression. They virtually never begin with the fact of sexual acts, then ask after their moral meanings, permissibilities, and limits. Margaret Farley's book, *Personal Commitments,*[60] attests this direction of thought in that it above all sets the *context* for speaking of sexual morality, the required prelude to any discourse about the specifics. Implicitly following through on Farley's agenda, Kay Zappone affirms, in her treatment of feminist spirituality:

> At the heart of sexual intimacy . . . is the desire
> to wholly express and nurture the mutuality of
> committed relationship. Commitment . . . re-

quires the same kind of vulnerability, openness, risk-taking, and trust at the level of genital sexuality as it does within every other
dimension of the partnership.[61]

It is evident, then, that in women's theological writing, sex as an act or activity tends to be subsumed within
a more holistic relational view. A final important illustration is Mary Hunt's *Fierce Tenderness*.[62] This work is
distinctive because Hunt writes from a lesbian Christian
perspective, providing a focused lens through which to
view *women's* friendship, and *women's* sexuality. Calling
"generativity" across a variety of social spheres the
"hallmark of friendship," Hunt describes a model in
which friendship is defined by love, power (as the ability
to make choices), embodiment, and spirituality.[63]

Lesbianism as genital sexual activity is not especially high on the book's program; Hunt's concern is
not with the justification as such of sexual acts among
women. Nor does she even begin with sexual phenom-
ena in general, and ask which forms of sexual expression can or cannot ever represent or achieve friendship.
Instead, Hunt begins with the nature of friendship, seen
through the experience of women. She then pursues
the theme of embodiment toward contemplation of
what love of friendship means if friendship is a form of
relationality among embodied and physical selves. The
terms Hunt uses to display the daily texture of embodied love have an affinity with the theory that sex is, after
all, an extension of humanity's linguistic ability, of the
human capacity to use symbols, gestures, signs, to dis-
close heart and mind, and to evoke participative re-

sponse from others. This symbolic capacity and need pervade every aspect of human existence and tinge with interpersonal relationality every instant of our embodied presence with others, especially our friends.[64]

In friendship, we maintain and try to enhance the relationship despite its and our own inevitable imperfections, and despite the need for closure to some other opportunities for intimacy, opportunities which we could not realize without shortchanging the good of the friendship in which we have already chosen to invest. Margaret Farley comments that commitments limit future choices as we choose again and again to ratify our commitments in concrete ways, thus actualizing options which otherwise could remain only potentialities. "Insofar as the commitment remains binding, my new choices are qualified as choices of fidelity or betrayal."[65] Yet while commitment limits the process by which we define ourselves in relationships with a future, it is also what makes this process possible. Farley does not venture into specific discussions of sexual morality. But the implication of her angle on relationships is that sexual expression should emerge within some relationships as a further refinement and prolongation of commitment, a commitment to this friendship and not some other, a specification of friendship which is also an enabling of its future development.

SEX-BASED GENDER DIFFERENCES: NATURE OR NURTURE?

The special prominence of intimacy and even committed friendship in the writings of women about sexuality lead ineluctably to the question whether the female sexual experience is different than the male to a degree which would make its repercussions in our affective, emotional, social, and even cognitive lives fairly profound. I have often been struck by the likelihood that Augustine's fearful anxieties about whether God's intentions for the human creature could really be compatible with reproduction by means of "the shameful motions of the organs of generation" reflect the male experience of sexual arousal much more than the female. Augustine obviously had both personal and philosophical dilemmas in interpreting sexual feelings which he felt unable to bring under full rational control. Today, a sense of humor may provide the most appropriate approach to this Church Father's musings about whether, if Adam and Eve had remained unblemished by sin, God would have found a more dignified way to continue the race than through genital sexual response.[66] But in contrast to Augustine, recent women's literature on sex and theology centers much less (or not at all) on sexual desire and its culmination in intercourse. The latter more specific concerns may be much more natural for persons (i.e., men?) whose sexual experience is physiologically more focused, intense, and often less physically controllable, even in the interests of physical arousal's morally attractive "relational potential."

In addition to sexual response, another area of difference in women's and men's embodied sexuality is in the area of parenthood. At least historically and to date, only women can be pregnant and give birth. In most cultures of the world, women have been primarily responsible for infant care. Young children are typically dependent on their mother's lactation, perhaps the clearest instance of a social-role creating biological function. In other animal species, hormonally-triggered "nurturing behavior" characterizes mothers in relation to offspring, so that essentially biological roles are determined and socialized through complementary emotional responses. Are human mothers—or even all women—also destined by biological sex differences to assume certain characteristically "feminine" social roles?

The insurmountable barrier to a clear and final answer to this question is the impossibility of obtaining for observation any pure, unsocialized specimen of either female or male humanity. The "nature/nurture" question provides the axis of a critical exploration of the problem, rather than the alternatives of an answer. In her now well-known studies of girls' and women's moral self-understanding, Carol Gilligan has demonstrated that, *de facto,* gender differences which correlate femininity with relationality rather than with impartial detachment do exist.[67]

Based on pastoral and counseling experience, the Whiteheads outline typical male and female approaches to sexuality which divide along similar lines. For instance, they say, women tend to find close relationships essential, satisfying, and even a source of security. For men, on the other hand, emotional security comes from independence, and relationships can be threatening to their sense of self.[68] In friendships, women tend to seek self-disclosure, while men seek camaraderie, and this spills over into their sexual expectations.[69] Women respond to friendship first at the emotional level, and "look forward to connecting with" another person "in experiences of empathy, care, and companionship." Only subsequently are women open to the possibility of sexual intimacy in certain friendships. Hence, "for most women, emotional closeness comes before and opens the way for genital love." But men often "experience these two aspects of eros in the reverse order: for them sexual attraction comes before and opens the way to a deeper emotional connection."[70] In much the same mode as Gilligan, the Whiteheads describe differences that *actually* exist, rather than arguing that such discrepancies are *naturally* necessary.

Other authors addressing Christian sexuality go further, frequently building upon Jungian archetypes of the feminine and masculine. John Dwyer, for instance, repudiates oppression of women, but still is sympathetic to the idea that "there are real personality differences which account for the differences in views, interests, and values between men and women." There is, perhaps, even "an essential altruism (concern for the other) that belongs to the very nature of a woman." Seeming to inscribe behavioral differences into a universal female nature, Dwyer suggests that "women are far more concerned with life in its totality, with all aspects of life, and that they have a natural desire to create a stable and secure environment for those around them." Moreover, women are "more deeply concerned about personal relationships" and they "tend toward a more intuitive kind of knowing."[71]

But the strong *social* emphasis on women's traditional role as nurturer may have been the primary influence in encouraging their development of virtues such as compassion and self-sacrifice, as well as greater attentiveness to the relational dimensions of human realities in general. Recent social scientific, especially anthropological, studies suggest that culture is at least as influential in biology in determining social conceptions of appropriate traits and behavior for men and women.[72] As two feminist anthropologists have recently stated;

> . . . natural features of gender, and natural processes of sex and reproduction, furnish only a suggestive and ambiguous backdrop to the cultural organization of gender and sexuality. What gender is, what men and women are, what sorts of relations do or should obtain between them—all of these notions do not simply reflect or elaborate upon biological "givens," but are largely products of social and cultural processes. The very emphasis on the biological factor within different cultural traditions is variable; some cultures claim that male-female differences are almost entirely biologically grounded, whereas others give biological differences, or supposed biological differences, very little emphasis.[73]

Examples given of the cultural pliability of gender range from institutionalized male cross-dressing and homosexuality (the *berdache*) in Native North American cultures; to the conflictual social and sexual roles which divide men and women in Andalusia, leading men to fear women and to characterize them with demonic symbolism; to the relatively free and mutually respectful sexual activity of Polynesia, which, however, is shadowed by frequent rape and the strong subordination of married women in the domestic sphere.

It may be going too far to imply the conclusion that gender roles are entirely "constructed" upon a biological substratum to which they bear no intrinsic connection whatsoever. For one thing, even though there may be cross-cultural variation, the incidence of patriarchal societies is certainly much higher than those which are even relatively egalitarian or which define sex in some mode other than the procreative one oriented toward male lineage concerns. But there is good evidence to think that whatever sex-based differences may exist in "natural" male and female experiences of the world hardly destine women (and *not men*), through their sexuality, either to social roles of domesticity and child nurturance or to sexual and moral roles of relationality, empathy and compassion (as correlatively *unnatural for men*).

Only a small number of emotional and cognitive sex differences are scientifically well-substantiated. Eleanor Maccoby and Carol Jacklin contend that most stereotypical assumptions about male and female psychological characteristics lack an innate base. They do, however, accept four differences as statistically significant: verbal ability in girls, and mathematical ability, visual spatial ability, and aggression in boys. Yet even in these cases, the variation within each gender is even greater than the difference between men and women. Moreover, consistent and "innate" nurturing behavior in human females has not been documented.[74]

Psychologist Nancy Chodorow offers a theoretical explanation of how gender roles can be so consistently perpetuated across cultures if they are not absolutely universal and innate. The hegemony of typical gender expectations depends on the virtually exclusive assignment of women to the care of small children.[75] If every individual's primary childhood contact is with the mother, then men will experience growth to maturity as a separation requiring assertive independence, while women will experience it as a relational continuum of interdependence. Of course, this theory also assumes that women's nurturing already exists within a larger social system of separate gender roles for men and women. For, not only does the male child have to separate from the mother, but he has to imitate a male role which entails completely different kinds of activities, emotions, and self-understandings than those with which he has been enabled to become familiar throughout early childhood.

In her widely noted book, *Maternal Thinking*, philosopher Sara Ruddick turns reflective attention again to the concrete experience of mothering, an activity which she does not see as the exclusive province of females.[76] In many ways, she offers a contemporary feminist "re-visioning" of Aquinas' method, for she wants to tie moral insights to the engendering experiential realities, while at the same time provoking critiques of both. Ruddick's ultimate agenda is to cultivate the parental experience as a storehouse of the sort of radical and reliable human empathy required to overcome the race's violent, war-prone tendencies. But her preliminary and in its own right valuable contribution is to elucidate some universals in the claims children make on parents, claims that the very being of a child makes for preservation of life and for nurturance. These claims evoke and sustain the passionate parental invest- ment ("mothering") which Ruddick describes in terms of "attentive love." "Clear-sighted attachment, loving clear-sightedness, is the aim, guiding principle, and cor- rective of maternal thinking. . . . Maternal attention is prompted by the responsibility to act and, when it is most successful, gives way to the action it informs."[77]

An ambivalence in Ruddick's thought surrounds the issue of the specifically female founts of maternal responsiveness. Although she holds it up as an ideal for both genders, she seems torn by a need to recognize that women's (and men's) embodiment gives their pa- rental experience a distinctive coloration or at least foundation. For instance, "women tend to know, in a way and to a degree that many men do not, both the history and the cost of human flesh." This is partly due to their *historically* greater involvement in "the work of mothering." But it can also derive partly "from an expe- rience or appreciation of female birthing labor on which all subsequent mothering depends."[78]

This brings us back to the enigma of gender differ- ence in the definition of sexual identity and reproduc- tive roles. As has no doubt become evident by now, I have no magic wand that will allow us to dissolve this quandary once and for all. My partial and provisional wisdom on the subject consists in a persistent, low-level warning noise rather than a constructive, high-flown paradigm shift. To be embodied as human beings means that we can accept no jarring dualism between physical capacities and psychospiritual and social accomplishments. At the same time, our embodiment is so thoroughly historical, that we must be ever-wary of assertions that any particular cultural mediation of the body's meaning is a "given" of nature and of human fate. Biology is not destiny. Neither is freedom disincarnate.

5.
A CRITICAL RETRIEVAL
OF THE CATHOLIC PROPOSAL

We have seen that feminist reinterpretations of the biblical literature on sex and gender, and a renewed reliance on sexual "experience" in normative moral reflection, have offered tremendous resources for reconstructing a Catholic tradition on women and sexuality which in the past was built primarily on natural law. After particular consideration of the experience of intimacy as a source of sexual ethics, we have assessed some efforts of the current pope, John Paul II, to retrieve and renew this same tradition for a contemporary audience. Official Catholic thought on sexuality today is aimed to recognize not only procreation, but also mutuality and the goodness of sexual love. Yet it still has patriarchal implications for women, whose basic identity is defined in relation to their childbearing and nurturing function within the family. Hence, revisionist suggestions within this tradition must be informed by the feminist critique. Our conclusion will be an effort to restate constructively the Catholic approach to sexuality in a way that could be fruitful in shaping discourse toward a more integral, embodied, and social perception of sex's meaning, and which applies essentially the same interpretive framework for men and women.

Catholic revisionist thought about sexuality often or even typically reacts against what can only be described as a "pre-Vatican II" mind-set, in which sexual morality was defined in terms of procreative acts in marriage. The narrowness of this vision and the scrupulosity and guilt it perpetrated among Catholics certainly deserve to be repudiated. However, Catholics born during or after the council no longer have the same need for "liberation" from a repressive sexual ethos.

If we consider the current North American *cultural* ambience, then reassurances to young adults like "Sex is good—a simple statement and yet one often disputed"; or, "Despite our negative experience, the Christian conviction stands: the body is holy; sex is good; God dwells here,"[79] seem not only anachronistic but irrelevant. Young Catholics are confronting a culture in which "value-free" encouragements to sexual enjoyment, combined with peer pressure to trade sex for status, leave a trail of confusion about how to formulate any sexual norms at all which go beyond individual preference and free consent. While pre-Vatican II Catholics needed to discover intimacy in order to transcend the biological/functional, procreation-centered view of sex within Catholic culture, post-Vatican II Catholics need to recover both intimacy and the parental potential of sex in order to offset the sex drive/individualist, gratification-centered view of it. Just as surely as did the older model, but in an opposite way, this newer cultural ethos overwhelms the sense that sex is *personal* and *relational*.

It is in its affirmation that sexual union, psychological and emotional intimacy, and shared parenthood are interdependent and mutually reinforcing realities that Catholicism has a message for our broader cultural ethic of sexuality. The necessary correction to the traditional way of stating this unity is to add that the three "Catholic" values of sex, love, and procreation are all to be understood as ongoing *personal relationships,* rather than as isolated acts or qualities of acts. And, as against common cultural assumptions, these relationships are not three essentially separable "options," but are intrinsically interconnected. Catholicism's prophetic ideal—that personal commitment, sexual expression, and shared parental creativity are mutually integral ongoing relationships—does *not* yield a simple new code of specific sexual behavior. Ideals for sexuality, as for other spheres of moral relationship, must be translated into practical reality with prudence and sensitivity to the limits of the human condition. However, the prophetic ideal should always inform evaluative thinking about sexual conduct and relationships, and should somehow be operative in specific conclusions.

A further specification of the ideal helps to move toward the resolution of at least some conflict cases. The three values of sexual intimacy, committed love, and parenthood can be prioritized, with loving commitment in the first place as the one inviolable value. The realization of the other two values is more contingent on material and physical conditions, and hence will be difficult or impossible to fulfill in certain circumstances, such as impotence, infertility or a homosexual orientation. Hence, sexual expression and shared biological parenthood can, at least in some instances, be sacrificed to the priority of the love relationship of the couple.

At the same time, sexual love is always an *embodied* love. Therefore, a loving intention is not the sole or sufficient criterion of even a revised sexual morality. To allow "love" or "freedom" exclusive control of decisions in sexual morality would be as dualistic as to absolutize as a moral norm the physical structure of sexual acts. Morally responsible sexual behavior must continue to seek to realize the sacrificed values, if not now, then at a later point in the relationship. For instance, the couple who used birth control to limit parenthood now, may still seek that role at other points in the relationship. The couple who relies on technology rather than intercourse to conceive a child will still express their mutual and procreative love sexually at other times. However, I would say that both the use of third party or "donor" forms of infertility therapy, and the view that parenthood is *per se* an optional aspect of marriage are excluded by the moral ideal.

New Reproductive Ventures

The new reproductive technologies have given us a new twist on *Humanae vitae's* triad of sex, love, and procreation. They make it possible for "sex" to become one of several separable components, rather than the "given" point of departure for the moral analysis. Beyond this, technologies offer new means, without sexual intercourse, for unmarried partners to create children together and to plan from the start to raise them apart. These new ventures differ from the classic adoption case in that they are not remedial interventions into a preexisting situation; they are deliberate initiatives in which at least one of the biological parents enters the process with the premeditated purpose of producing an offspring in relation to whom all his or her parental ties are rejected. Donor insemination, a widely used technique, has made it possible for decades for couples to combat male infertility by using third party "anonymous" sperm. A growing number of unmarried women today choose donor insemination in order to bear their own biological child outside of a personal relationship to the father. And now the use of donor ova has also entered the picture.

Perhaps the most notorious challenge to women's reproductive role has been presented by surrogate motherhood, in which a woman typically accepts money to bear a child with someone else's husband, then relinquishes that child to the couple. In the "Baby M" case, a dispute arose subsequent to the birth of the child, which forced consideration of the premise that "motherhood" (or "parenthood") is a relation whose existence depends entirely on free consent to a contract, and can by contract be irrevocably severed. An equally bothersome aspect of such cases, from a feminist point of view, is their potential to co-opt the reproductive services— and indeed the children—of poor, immigrant, and minority women driven by economic desperation. The parameters of "motherhood" are stretched further when we read of an increasing number of cases in which women act as "host uteruses" for the embryos of their biological relatives, often sisters or daughters. (A crucial difference here is that, unlike the surrogate motherhood agreements, the "donor" is not the biological mother of a child which she signs away, but a prenatal care-giver for a child who has two other biological parents.)

The revisionist Catholic approach I am proposing will not be able to settle all the reproductive "hard cases" once and for all. Some gray areas are no doubt going to be part of the moral picture in sex and reproduction, as in everything else in life. Rather than focusing primarily on the limits of reproductive choices, I want to address the general ethos about the meaning and value of parenthood out of which this quickly expanding variety of "options" emerges.

Proponents of these new technologies usually emphasize good results that can be gained, free consent of participants, and the importance of parental love for the child. Freedom and rights in relation to parenthood are crucial parts of the rhetoric. Opponents, on the other hand—definitely in the cultural minority—invest "natural" biological relationships with a good deal more importance, and tend to assume that the interpersonal relationships of family and parenthood should correspond to biogenetic substructures. On the one side, the rhetoric holds up autonomy and self-determination; on the other, it holds up human biological nature and God as its designer, as well as the inviolability of traditional family forms. The first side, which is pro-technology and sees parenthood as contractual, is the expression of a politically liberal and individualist ethos focused on individual rights and privacy.

The second, well-captured by the teaching of the Roman Catholic Church, is focused on biologically-based conceptions of "nature," and tends to see infertility (or difficulty in locating a spouse-parent partner) as a form of human suffering to which, after certain moderate forms of resistance, the appropriate response is resignation.

In the first, liberal, view, it is choice and contract that determine parenthood, and the law should serve as a social mechanism for guaranteeing the protection of choice. According to liberal feminist and lawyer Lori B. Andrews, "it is important to choose a primary family for the infant before his or her birth. One approach would be to have a policy that always holds that the intended parents are the legal parents."[80] Adopting a more utilitarian mode of analysis to arrive at similar conclusions about the acceptability of surrogacy, Ruth B. Macklin asserts that counterarguments that focus on "exploitation" and "dehumanization" do not meet her criterion of "probable beneficial and harmful consequences."[81]

However, the 1987 Vatican *Instruction* on reproductive technologies represents a fundamentally different moral approach to either the liberal or the utilitarian one. Scientific interventions into reproduction "must be at the service of the human person," and of "his true and integral good according to the design and will of God," a good deriving from "the special nature of the human person."[82] Upholding the criterion of *Humanae vitae*, i.e., that sex, love, and conception be united in "each and every act" of intercourse, the *Instruction* outlaws not only donor methods, but also any techniques used in marriage which eliminate the sexual act as the means of conception. Echoing the vocabulary of John Paul II, the document continues, "In order to respect the language of their bodies and their natural generosity, the conjugal union must take place with respect for its openness to procreation; and the procreation of a person must be the fruit and the result of married love."[83] The Vatican also urges governments to enact laws ensuring that this standard of conception-through-sex-in-marriage will be met.

Many Catholics, not to mention their fellow citizens, find this line of attack unconvincing. Most perceive a difference larger than the Vatican allows between therapies used in marriage, even if they do temporarily circumvent sexual intercourse, and methods which bring donors into the marital procreative venture. I believe that donor methods are more morally objectionable because they do not appreciate the unity as *relationships* of sexual expression, committed partnership, and parenthood, all of which are embodied as well as intentional and free. Both surrogacy and artificial insemination deny any real connection of biological reproduction either to social parenthood or to a commitment to one's reproductive partner. Instead, they rely on a basic denial of the material and physical preconditions of moral obligation in general, and of parenthood in particular. But the mutual obligations created by kinship—especially among children, parents, and siblings—are moral bonds that persons cannot simply "decide" into nonexistence.

In a recent edition of the *Washington Post*, there appeared an article on "single mothers by choice."[84] It revealingly displayed the awkward position of women in a culture which affirms free choice as the key constitu-ent of moral agency, and, somewhat paradoxically, still holds up biological motherhood as a role without which women remain incomplete. Most of the women inter-viewed would have chosen marriage were it available to them. Missing that option, they have taken matters into their own hands, asserting for instance that it is not necessary "to defend my position to strangers." The bottom line was clarified by a Richmond nurse with six-year-old twin boys: "As the years went on and I got older, I knew it was important for me to have a child." All the women interviewed delighted in their children and most were at peace with their decision, regardless of social difficulties and more-than-occasional insensitive remarks. But one woman, with a fifteen-year-old son, gives this advice to other prospective single mothers: "I would say adopt. Don't grow your own from the selfish perspective that you want this. The cost to the child is high."

I concur in this woman's preference for adoption over a contract with a stranger who intends never to know his child. Many children worldwide are in much more desperate need of families than these educated, successfully employed women are of pregnancy and genetically-related offspring. Nonetheless, I find it dif-ficult to judge that the motive of most single mothers is "selfish." I see the problem more in terms of the values that our culture holds up for emulation, and of the moral blind spots which its endorsement of these same values perpetuates. These women are not selfish, but they *are* pragmatic and individualist. They construe morality primarily in terms of free choice and "taking control" of their options. Our culture has a remarkably low tolerance for accepting the hardships of life as part of a search for other alternatives, and does little to encourage the resolution of one's own suffering through the alleviation of the suffering of others. Women (and men) in our culture are thus encouraged to attach their quite natural desire for a "biological" child to their self-concept as a free and autonomous person. The morally admirable individual derives personal and social worth from the amount of control exercised over adverse circumstances, and the degree to which he or she can succeed in meeting personal objectives, no matter what the obstacles.

A different ethos might encourage identification with the needs of parentless children already in existence, and the relinquishment of one's aspiration to experience pregnancy in favor of the welcoming of a child who otherwise might never know maternal love at all. Such an alternative ethos would value biogenetic parenthood, as I have done throughout this essay in relation to sexuality's significance. But it might also affirm the ideal of keeping in unity the sexual, the committed, and the parental relations, insofar as they are both personal and embodied, and would also discourage their deliberate rupture as a personal or policy choice. My point is not so much to condemn women or couples who resort to donor methods, usually with good intentions. It is to ask whether good intentions and personal satisfaction are adequate moral standards. I want to raise deeper questions about attitudes toward sexuality and parenthood which inhibit our ability to see methods which join strangers in procreation as even morally problematic.

Sex is fundamentally and above all a relational capacity, and the relationships it implies include not only the sexual partners, but also children, family, and society. The relationships among physical sex, personal partnership, and parenthood as the outcome of sex, form a moral unity, and in this unity consists the moral meaning of sexuality. "Reproduction" is not a capacity which can be understood apart from the context of human sexuality as relational vis-a-vis both the child and the co-parent. The relationality of sex is fulfilled most perfectly in the parenthood of spouses, situated within an intergenerational family network which opens out onto and participates in the common good of the community as a whole.

To conclude, women's experience of sexuality, given both its biological and its historical contours, should well attune us to the potential of sex to be *parental*—not in the narrow sense of "procreation," but in the sense of an ongoing social bond of nurturance and love. Our experience of sexuality also includes a sense of its power for *intimacy* and union, grounding shared family life. These values are not values only for women. But women can affirm their value for men on the basis of what has already been their greater realization in women's lives. Women's sexuality can be a window onto the elemental meanings of human sexuality: it finds its meaning through the mutuality of partners in sexual desire and fulfillment; in the durable, intimate friendship enhanced by "tenderness" (Ricoeur); and in the arduous but delightful procreativity of sex, an avenue for mother and father to share "attentive love" and care (Ruddick), a love as bounteous in human meaning as the sexual and spousal bond.

NOTES

1. ST. I-II. Q 94. a 2.
2. Ibid., I-II. Q 94. a. 4.
3. Ibid., II-II. Q. 154. a 12.
4. See Augustine, "The Good of Marriage," in *The Fathers of the Church, Volume 15: St. Augustine, Treatises on Marriage and Other Subjects*, ed. Ray J. Deferrari (NY: Fathers of the Church, Inc., 1955) 3–51; and Thomas Aquinas, *Summa Theologica Suppl.* (NY: Benziger Brothers, 1948) Q. 49, "The Marriage Goods."
5. ST. I. Q. 92. a 1.
6. For a scholarly argument that the egalitarian community of disciples which Jesus established was gradually eroded by the accommodationism of the early church, see Elisabeth Schüssler Fiorenza, *In Memory of Her: A Feminist Theological Reconstruction of Christian Origins* (NY: Crossroad, 1983).
7. *On the Goods of Marriage,* nos. 6–7; ST. Suppl. Q 41. a 4.
8. "Home and Work: Women's Roles and the Transformation of Values," in Walter Burghardt, ed., *Woman: New Dimensions* (NY/Ramsey/Toronto: Paulist Press, 1975) 71–83.
9. ST Suppl. Q. 41. a 3.
10. ST II-II. Q 26. a 11; and *Summa Contra Gentiles* (Notre Dame: University of Notre Dame Press, 1975) 3/II. 123.6.
11. *Women and the Word* (New York/Mahwah: Paulist Press,

1986). See also Letty M. Russell, ed., *Feminist Interpretation of the Bible* (Philadelphia: Westminster, 1985).

12. Raymond F. Collins, *Christian Morality: Biblical Foundations* (Notre Dame IN: University of Notre Dame Press, 1986) 176.

13. Collins, *Christian Morality,* 169.

14. Phyllis Trible, *Texts of Terror: Literary-Feminist Readings of Biblical Narratives.* (Philadelphia: Fortress Press, 1984).

15. The leading source here has been Phyllis Trible, *God and the Rhetoric of Sexuality* (Philadelphia: Fortress Press, 1978).

16. "Women in the Bible and Its World," *Interpretation* 42/7 (1988) 42.

17. See, for instance, Halvor Moxnes, *The Economy of the Kingdom: Social Conflict and Economic Relations in Luke's Gospel* (Philadelphia: Fortress Press, 1988).

18. Perkins, "Women in the Bible," 44.

19. See Victor Paul Furnish, *The Moral Teaching of Paul: Selected Issues,* second edition (Nashville: Abingdon, 1985) 101–14.

20. Cf. Furnish, *Moral Teaching,* 94–101.

21. Furnish, *Moral Teaching,* 90–92.

22. Schüssler Fiorenza, *In Memory of Her,* 262–63.

23. Elisabeth Schüssler Fiorenza, "Toward a Feminist Biblical Hermeneutics: Biblical Interpretation and Liberation Theology, in Charles E. Curran and Richard A. McCormick, eds., *The Use of Scripture in Moral Theology* (New York: Paulist, 1984) 375.

24. Ibid., 376. See also *In Memory of Her,* 32.

25. *In Memory of Her,* 33. See also, "Feminist Hermeneutics," 376.

26. *Slavery, Sabbath, War, and Women: Case Issues in Biblical Interpretation* (Scottdale PA; Kitchener, Ontario: Herald Press, 1983).

27. Ibid., 146.

28. Ibid., 190.

29. Ibid., 232.

30. Letty M. Russell, "Authority and the Challenge of Feminist Interpretation," in *Feminist Hermeneutics*, 144.

31. See Cahill, *Between the Sexes*, 4–7.

32. James M. Gustafson, *Theology and Christian Ethics* (Philadelphia: Pilgrim Press, 1974) 144.

33. "The critical principle of feminist theology is the promotion of the full humanity of women. Whatever denies, diminishes, or distorts the full humanity of women is, therefore, appraised as not redemptive. Theologically speaking, whatever diminishes or denies the full humanity of women must be presumed not to reflect the divine or an authentic relation to the divine, or to reflect the authentic nature of things, or to be the message or work of an authentic redeemer or a community of redemption" (*Sexism and God-Talk: Toward a Feminist Theology* [Boston: Beacon Press, 1983] 18–19).

34. Margaret A. Farley, "Sexual Ethics," *Encyclopedia of Bioethics, Volume 4*, ed. Warren T. Reich (New York: Macmillan Publishing Co., Inc.) 1585.

35. Ibid., 1587.

36. "Wonder, Eroticism and Enigma," *Cross Currents* 14 (1964) 136–37.

37. *The Sexual Language: An Essay in Moral Theology* (Ottawa: University of Ottawa, 1976). See also Bernard Haring, *Free and Faithful in Christ, Vol. 2, The Truth Will Set You Free* (New York: Seabury, 1979) 504.

38. Vincent Genovesi, S.J., *In Pursuit of Love: Catholic Morality and Human Sexuality* (Wilmington DL: Michael Glazier, 1987) 141.

39. John C. Dwyer, *Human Sexuality: A Christian View* (Kansas City: Sheed and Ward, 1987) 48.

40. *Pius XI on Christian Marriage: The English Translation* (New York: Barry Vail Corporation, 1931) 12.

41. *Gaudium et spes (The Documents of Vatican II,* ed., Walter

M. Abbott, S. J. [New York: America Press, 1966]) no.
51.

42. Paul VI, *Humanae vitae* (Paramus NJ: Paulist Press, 1968)
no. 7.

43. For a review of Catholic sexual ethics in the last half century, which elaborates the factors contributing to change
in greater detail, see Lisa Sowle Cahill, "Catholic Sexual
Ethics and the Dignity of the Person: A Double Message," *Theological Studies* 50 (1989) 120–50.

44. See Dietrich von Hildebrand, *Marriage* (New York: Long-
mans, 1942; originally *Die Ehe* (Munich: Kosel-Oustet,
1929); and Herbert Doms, *The Meaning of Marriage* (New
York: Sheed and Ward, 1939); originally *Vom Sinn und
Zweck der Ehe* (Breslau: Ostdeutsche Verlagsanstalt,
1935).

45. *Humanae vitae*, no. 9.

46. Ibid., no. 11.

47. Ibid., no. 13.

48. John Paul II, Reflections on *Humanae Vitae; Conjugal Morality and Spirituality* (Boston: St. Paul Editions, 1984) no.
30.

49. Ibid., no. 6.

50. John Paul II, *Original Unity of Man and Woman: Catechesis
on the Book of Genesis* (Boston: St. Paul; Editions, 1981)
111.

51. John Paul II, *On the Family* (Washington, D.C.: United
States Catholic Conference, 1982), no. 38.

52. Ibid., no. 32.

53. Ibid., no. 23.

54. *Mulieris Dignitatem* (*On the Dignity and Vocation of Women,*
1988), *Origins* 18 (1988) 261–83.

55. Ibid., no. 18.

56. Ibid., nos. 18, 28–30.

57. "The Church and Its Public Life," *America* 160 (1989)
553–54.

58. *A Sense of Sexuality: Christian Love and Intimacy* (New York, London, Toronto, Sydney, Auckland: Doubleday, 1989).

59. Ibid., 167–68.

60. San Francisco: Harper and Row, 1986.

61. Katherine E. Zappone, *The Hope for Wholeness: A Spirituality for Feminists* (Mystic CT: Twenty-Third Publications, 1991) 82.

62. Mary E. Hunt, *Fierce Tenderness: A Feminist Theology of Friendship* (New York: Crossroad, 1991).

63. Ibid., 98–99.

64. "Being with friends is the clearest way to understand embodiment. How else could we be except in the finitude of our physical selves? This is why touch and communication are so crucial. We say things without words to friends. Gestures, glances, silence, smiles take on shared meanings with intimates. Sexual relations are usually most satisfying when carried out between close friends. A meal, sports, prayer, work, theater are all heightened in the company of friends" (*Fierce Tenderness*, 82).

65. *Personal Commitments*, 44.

66. See *The City of God*, XIV. 19, 21, 23–24; and "The Good of Marriage," Chapter 2.

67. Carol Gilligan, *In a Different Voice: Psychological Theory and Women's Development* (Cambridge MA: Harvard University Press, 1982).

68. *A Sense of Sexuality*, 69–70.

69. Ibid., 173.

70. Ibid., 175.

71. *Human Sexuality*, 158–59. Dwyer relies on Lois and Joseph Bird, *The Freedom of Sexual Love* (New York: Doubleday, 1967); and Lois Clemens, *Woman Liberated* (Scottdale PA: Herald Press, 1971).

72. See Michelle Z. Rosaldo and Louise Lamphere, eds.,

Women, Culture, and Society (Stanford CA: Stanford University Press, 1975).

73. Sherry B. Ortner and Harriet Whitehead, "Introduction: Accounting for Sexual Meanings," in Ortner and Whitehead, eds., *Sexual Meanings: The Cultural Construction of Gender and Sexuality* (Cambridge/London/New York: Cambridge University Press, 1981) 1.

74. *The Psychology of Sex Differences* (Stanford CA: Stanford University Press, 1974). For a review of related literature, see Barbara Hilkert Andolsen, "Gender and Sex Roles in Recent Religious Ethics Literature," *Religious Studies Review* 11/3 (1985) 217–220, 222–223.

75. *The Reproduction of Mothering: Psychoanalysis and the Sociology of Gender* (Berkeley: University of California Press, 1978).

76. *Maternal Thinking: Toward a Politics of Peace* (Boston: Beacon Press, 1989).

77. Ibid., 122.

78. Ibid., 186.

79. Whitehead, *A Sense of Sexuality*, 22, 23.

80. "Feminist Perspectives on Reproductive Technologies," unpublished conference paper, 40. (Available from the author: Lori B. Andrews, American Bar Foundation, 750 Lake Shore Drive, Chicago, IL 60611.)

81. "Is There Anything Wrong with Surrogate Motherhood? An Ethical Analysis," *Law Medicine and Health Care* 16 (1988) 64.

82. Congregation for the Doctrine of the Faith, *Instruction on Respect for Human Life in Its Origin and on the Dignity of Procreation: Replies to Certain Questions of the Day, Origins* 16 (1987) "Introduction," 2, 4.

83. Ibid., II.B.4.

84. David Streitfeld, "When Baby Makes Two: Deciding to Have a Child Without a Husband," *Washington Post,* November 12, 1991, D5.